Scurry Through the Bustling World of
CITY ANIMALS

Published by Wildlife Education, Ltd.
12233 Thatcher Court, Poway, California 92064
contact us at: **1-800-477-5034**
e-mail us at: **animals@zoobooks.com**
visit us at: **www.zoobooks.com**

ISBN 978-1-888153-64-4

City Animals

Series Created by
John Bonnett Wexo

Written by
Marjorie Betts Shaw

Contents

Wild animals in the city?   6–7

Some animals visit cities   8–9

When cities grow   10–11

It's hard to believe   14–15

Partnerships   16–17

Getting to know wild animals   18–19

Visit animals in their natural habitats   20–21

Some of the animals that share   22–23

Index   24

Wild animals in the city? At first thought, this sounds unlikely. But in cities all over the world, some wild animals have made their homes.

Cities grow to make room for more people, and houses are often built in what was once wild country. When this happens, some animals retreat farther into the countryside, but others stay and learn to adapt to their new neighbors. We are so used to seeing some of these wild residents that they don't seem at all like wild animals.

We expect to see squirrels and chipmunks in city parks and in our backyards. The ducks and geese that swim in city lakes and ponds seem to belong there. We put feeders out for hummingbirds, sparrows, linnets, wrens, and other small birds. And pigeons and doves are part of city life in cities all over the world.

When these animals seem so familiar and so tame, why do we call them wild animals? Because these are not animals that have been domesticated, like your pet dog or cat. The wild animals can make their own way in the world and do not depend on humans for food, water, or affection. Yes, it may be easier for them to eat from your bird feeder or to raid your trash can, but these are only supplements to the wild animals' diets. They still can hunt for themselves and find the seed, pollen, and other foods they need in nature.

City animals vary depending on where they live in the world. In the western United States, cities might be surrounded by mountains, they may be located at the desert's edge, or they may crowd the seashore. Often these cities have canyons that run through them. Such cities provide a number of different habitats for wild animals. Cities in the northern, eastern, and southern parts of the United States have their own unique climates, habitats, and ecosystems that are suitable to different kinds of wildlife. For example, peregrine falcons like the view from the lofty heights of New York City skyscrapers. From there, they can dive into the deep canyons between tall buildings to swoop off with an unsuspecting pigeon.

In other parts of the world, some cities have animals that seem exotic to us, but are truly domestic, such as camels in India, Africa, and the Middle East. Depending on where you live, what kinds of wild animals do you see in your city or neighborhood? Wild rabbits? Lizards? Hawks? Deer? Raccoons? Foxes? Skunks? Alligators? Polar bears?

Black rhinos in Nairobi National Park ignore Nairobi's skyscrapers.

Some animals visit cities and other populated areas during winter "vacations" to warmer weather and more abundant food supplies. These migrants are much like people known as "snowbirds," who live in cold northern areas but winter in warmer climates. Some mammals, fish, and butterflies migrate, but it is usually migratory birds that stop in cities. A small flock of birds may descend on berry bushes in your backyard for a quick feast. Ducks, geese, and swans are attracted to local lakes, ponds, streams, or even decorative fountains and swimming pools!

One of the most popular migration stories tells of the swallows of Mission San Juan Capistrano in southern California. Since 1776, during the mission's earliest construction, cliff swallows have returned each spring.

Cliff swallows don't return just to Capistrano. They also return to barns, bridges, freeway overpasses, and homes across America. If, in spring, you see mud spattered on your front door or the side of your house, look up— you may have a swallow's nest under your eaves!

Wapiti (sometimes called North American elk) don't migrate long distances, but they do spend their summers in the mountains and move into the low valleys during winter. Fenced farmland and cattle ranches leave little room for wintering wapiti, though, and they are often forced to spend harsh winters in high mountain snows. These four wapiti have found a friendly service station in Canada's Jasper National Park, where they can fuel up by grazing on a grassy area.

ESSO   ESSO   ESSO

Polar bears have migrated through Churchill, Manitoba, since before the town was built in 1771. Instead of warmer weather, they look for colder climates, where they can hunt seals on the ice. From September through October, polar bears patrol Churchill, walking through houses and helping themselves to food. But their favorite place is the Churchill dump.

You are lucky if you live in the migration route of the monarch butterfly. If so, you may see thousands of them sleeping in neighborhood trees or on your house! They travel from Canada to Florida, California, and Mexico, where they winter.

Canada geese range the length and breadth of North America. When they migrate, they land on ponds, rivers, and streams in the wilderness or the heart of a city. In the Midwest they graze in farmers' wheat fields. In cities and suburbs, they bask on golf course waterways and are abundant in many city parks.

When cities grow and spread far into the countryside, they push wild residents from their habitats. This happens all over the world—from villages and cities in Africa and India to the suburbs of the western United States, which often cover the available land from the seashore to the mountains and into the desert. The borders between burgeoning city and dwindling wild space are where conflicts can occur between humans and wild animals.

People who live in subdivisions where the sprawling city spills into the country enjoy the country atmosphere. They like to see a hawk dive for prey alongside a busy freeway, but they're not so happy about a rattlesnake in the backyard, or that the cat is missing after a coyote was seen in the neighborhood. But coyotes, cougars, bobcats, and foxes were here first. This is life on the edge between city life and wildlife.

In Australia, big kangaroos go where they want. On city streets at night, they are often a traffic hazard. On the golf course, they pose a different kind of hazard when they nibble fairway grass while golfers tee off. Although the survival of many smaller kangaroos is threatened by encroaching civilization, the large kangaroos are numerous.

Human activities and habitat destruction account for about half of all deaths of the Florida manatee. Manatees get tangled in fishing line, swallow plastic bags and fishhooks, and get trapped in drainage culverts. But their biggest danger is the speedboat propeller. Most people in Florida are serious about saving their manatees. Wildlife agencies and countless volunteers educate the public about this vulnerable animal, warn boaters about manatees, and rescue and rehabilitate injured manatees. The purchase of manatee license plates helps to spread the message about manatees and provides funds to save this threatened marine mammal.

"Caution: Please brake for wildlife" could be the message here. This nesting pigeon keeps its eye on passersby.

When housing developments take over wild space, some animals are forced out. Other animals may stay and learn to coexist with the new "neighbors." Wild rabbits help themselves to plants in the neighborhood, and coyotes and foxes help themselves to the rabbits. Opossums, raccoons, and skunks clean up any food left out for domestic pets and happily forage in fruit trees. For the most part, nocturnal animals have the best chance of staying concealed and not being shooed away.

13

Canada geese on migration stop in Goshen, Connecticut.

It's hard to believe when you look at all the wild animals on these pages that, somewhere in the world, they all live close to humans. In the case of the water buffalo, there are still small populations of wild water buffaloes that live in several reserves in Asia. But the domestic forms of the water buffalo are widely distributed in East and Southeast Asia, South America, Europe, Japan, Hawaii, India, Pakistan, and North Africa. In these places they live and work alongside humans.

In Miami, Florida, diners at riverside restaurant terraces are warned away from the riverbanks with yellow police tape—a reminder that alligators like to dine too!

RED-TAILED HAWK
Farmlands, deserts, woodlands, cities and suburbs across North America.

HANUMAN LANGUR
From Afghanistan through India and Sri Lanka. Commonly seen in temples and towns.

WATER BUFFALO
A working companion to people around the world.

COUGAR, PUMA, OR MOUNTAIN LION
Southern Canada to Patagonia—ventures into towns and parks that border its wild habitat.

POLAR BEAR
The Arctic town of Churchill, Manitoba, posts signs that say "Polar Bears in Town: What to Do?"

GRAY SQUIRREL
Found in forested areas, in city parks, and in backyards.

MALLARD DUCK
Ponds, lakes, streams, in woodlands and in town and city parks.

NEW SOUTH WALES KOALA
Australian towns, cities, forests.

BLACK BEAR
The search for food brings these bears into contact with humans. They raid campgrounds, garbage dumps, and beehives.

ALLIGATOR LIZARD
Western half of United States. Near houses, this lizard lives in woodpiles, dense ground cover, bushes, and garages.

AMERICAN WOOD STORK
Florida swamps and marshes.

AMERICAN WHITE PELICAN
Marshes, lakes, seacoast towns and cities.

BOTTLE-NOSED DOLPHIN
Coastal waters and lagoons, where they often interact with boats, swimmers, and waders.

CALIFORNIA GULL
Seacoasts, lakes, farmlands along the Pacific Coast, northwest United States to mid-Canada.

BROWN BAT
In North America, roosts in caves, hollow trees, buildings, tunnels, wells, and backyard bat boxes.

ANNA'S HUMMINGBIRD
Parks, gardens, brushy open woodlands along the Pacific Coast of the United States.

MOOSE
(KNOWN AS ELK IN EUROPE)
May browse on ash, maple, and birch trees in northern yards and on aquatic plants in ponds. Seen on Alaskan airstrips, where they sometimes charge small planes.

GRAY KANGAROO
Australian plains, roads, backyards, and golf courses.

INDIAN COBRA
Found in rice paddies, city bazaars, villages, parks, gardens, sheds, and in homes.

GRAY FOX
At home in cities and towns with wild spaces nearby. May come into yards where food is available.

AMERICAN ALLIGATOR
Lakes and rivers of the Southeastern United States.

STRIPED SKUNK
North America. Many habitats, including the suburbs, where they live in burrows, under buildings, and in woodpiles.

BOBCAT
North America. Found in rocky hills, desert scrub, and the communities that adjoin these habitats.

COTTONTAIL
Occupies desert scrub, forest clearings, sand beaches, parks, and neighborhood gardens.

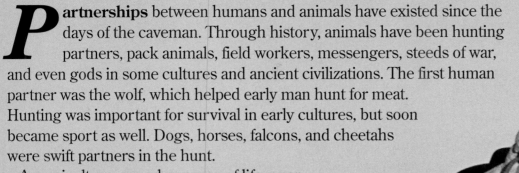

Partnerships between humans and animals have existed since the days of the caveman. Through history, animals have been hunting partners, pack animals, field workers, messengers, steeds of war, and even gods in some cultures and ancient civilizations. The first human partner was the wolf, which helped early man hunt for meat. Hunting was important for survival in early cultures, but soon became sport as well. Dogs, horses, falcons, and cheetahs were swift partners in the hunt.

As agriculture spread as a way of life, oxen and horses plowed the fields. Camels, llamas, and donkeys became pack animals. Elephants carried men to war and on tiger hunts.

From carrier pigeons to the Pony Express, animals have carried important messages for people. Since about 500 BC in China, pigeons have carried messages during war and peace and in medical emergencies and traffic jams.

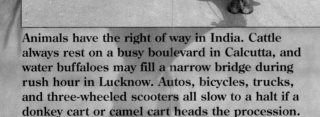

Animals have the right of way in India. Cattle always rest on a busy boulevard in Calcutta, and water buffaloes may fill a narrow bridge during rush hour in Lucknow. Autos, bicycles, trucks, and three-wheeled scooters all slow to a halt if a donkey cart or camel cart heads the procession.

A donkey loaded with baskets waits to carry laundry home in Mykonos, Greece.

A working elephant carries plant material along a road in Kerala State, India. Working elephants are often trained from infancy and develop a close relationship with their human partners.

Falconers spend many hours training their hunting partners. This Tunisian falconer depends on the bird-hunting skills of his peregrine falcon.

Some assistance dogs guide the blind, some lead a hearing-impaired person to a ringing telephone or doorbell, others may open doors, turn out the lights, get food from the refrigerator—the list of skills is endless. Although trained to help in different ways, these dogs all have one thing in common—their dependability, loyalty, and devotion to their human companions.

Hanuman langurs mingle with visitors to the Amber Palace in Jaipur, Rajasthan, India. These langurs are considered sacred in India. Legend tells that Hanuman and the king of the monkeys rescued a princess who had been kidnapped by an evil giant. The giant caught Hanuman and tried to set the monkey afire, but Hanuman put out the fire with his hands. The story says that is why all Hanuman langurs have black faces and hands.

Getting to know wild animals is fun. Besides reading about them or watching nature programs on television, you can invite them over!

Even in a high-rise apartment, you can hang bird feeders for seed-eating birds and for hummingbirds, which like nectar. A garden with bright-colored, deep-throated flowers will also draw nectar-eating birds. The birds you attract may feel safe enough to stay. If they build nests, you may see them feeding their young and teaching them to fly.

Depending on where you live, you might see rabbits or lizards in your yard. And at night, you might see an opossum or a raccoon or a bat. You might even hear an owl. Get to know the animals that live around you. Watch a spider spin its web. With a magnifying glass, you may be able to see the silk coming out of the spider's spinnerets. The secret to seeing wildlife in action is to stay alert and watch quietly.

Raccoons will raid your trash cans, but they may also arrive at your door to ask for a handout, like this family of raccoons in Washington. Be warned—once you feed them treats, they will return regularly and can be demanding!

As soon as there were humans, there were some animals ready to follow a domestic life. One of these was the house mouse. Long before there were "houses," the house mouse found it useful to live with humans, eat their grain, search through their garbage, and travel with them to all parts of the world.

This eastern gray squirrel in Berkeley Heights, New Jersey, is following in the footsteps of its ancestors—it's helping itself to the grain on a sheaf of oats. When the first colonists planted their plots of grain and corn, hundreds of thousands of gray squirrels left the forests and devoured the new crops.

Many people do not like to have skunks on their property. But the most important part of a skunk's diet is insects. They eat a host of insects and larvae that destroy plants. So, if a skunk wanders through your yard, don't startle it. Let it forage on your insect population and move on.

If you live in coyote country and leave dog food out or are plagued by rabbits, mice, or rats, a coyote may find its way to your door. Coyotes are skilled at pest control and help to keep the diseases in check that are spread by rodents. Just don't leave small dogs out with the dog food. Any animal that is small is fair game to the coyote.

The opossum is no stranger to towns and cities. Opossums may live in another animal's abandoned den or in your woodshed. They eat everything from food scraps to insects, snails, fruits, and vegetables. They forage at night, but if you're lucky, you might see them in the early evening or the early morning.

Visit animals in their natural habitats. You probably won't need to travel far outside your own community to discover new things about your wild neighbors.

Owls are probably closer to you than you ever imagined. The best time to search for owls is at dusk or at dawn. The owls you are most likely to find are the barn owl, the screech owl, and the great horned owl. Barn owls are as comfortable living in barns, church belfries, and your attic, as in the hollow of a tree.

If owls are present you will probably hear them hoooooooting or screeching. But you won't hear them flying, because they fly on silent wings to capture their prey. When you go "owling," be sure to take binoculars so you can get a close-up view.

If you live near the ocean in an area where whales migrate, or where they calve, you may be able to ride on an excursion boat to see the whales. The tourists in this boat are following a sperm whale off Kaikoura, New Zealand. The California gray whale is perhaps the best-known whale-watching subject. It follows the Pacific Coast of the United States to the calving lagoons of Baja California, Mexico.

You can invite bats to your yard by building a bat house or—if you know where a colony of bats lives—you can watch them take wing at twilight to hunt insects. If you live in Austin, Texas, you can be part of a summer event and take a picnic basket to join others for the nightly flight of Mexican freetail bats from beneath the Congress Avenue Bridge.

Where city limits extend to the foothills and the edge of the desert, to the southern swamps, or to the northern woodlands, bobcats may roam through an occasional yard or onto a highway that runs through town. Be alert if you see one cross in front of your car's headlights—the bobcat will be gone in a flash!

At a pond in a park, along a stream near your home, or at a local estuary, you may see turtles, fish, and a variety of water birds such as herons, egrets, and wood storks.

Some of the animals that share city life with humans aren't even natives of the land—they have been introduced. Native animals are often threatened when foreign wildlife is introduced into their habitats. People sometimes introduce new wildlife on purpose, but more often these new species get a free ride to a new land on a boat, in a suitcase, or even on someone's clothing! The clothes moth arrived in America with the Pilgrims. "Killer" bees were imported by ship from Africa to South America. They later escaped and flew on their own power into the United States.

However they get to their new destination, these invaders often conquer the native inhabitants, which have no defenses against the newcomers. And the newcomers have no enemies to halt their invasion, so they become fixtures in our environment. Sometimes people introduce animals hoping they will take care of a pest, only to discover they have created an even worse pest.

When people began to live in cities, the pest populations grew. There were more people, more food cupboards, and more garbage cans to attract these tiny residents to our homes. These city dwellers are survivors. Some were here 250 million years ago—long before humans arrived on the scene.

Some animals have adjusted very well to living close to people. And what some people enjoy seeing around their homes, other people consider pests. Skunks, raccoons, armadillos, opossums, and coyotes are some of these. Deer are so numerous in parts of the United States that they show up in surprising places. Several years ago some travelers were startled when an equally startled deer ran into a hotel lobby in the heart of Des Moines, Iowa. In some areas of the eastern United States deer are so bothersome that hunters have been encouraged to get their deer in residential backyards.

Now that humans and wildlife are sharing more and more of the same habitats, conflicts are bound to occur. One way to avoid conflicts is to provide wildlife corridors when new housing developments are built. These corridors allow animals to pass from one wild habitat to another, so the wild residents are not trapped in a human settlement. In the meantime, consider yourself lucky if you have wildlife nearby. It's a wonderful way to learn about nature in your own backyard.

White storks have found a lofty nesting spot at Neuruppin, a city near Berlin, Germany.

23

Index

Alligator lizard, 14
Alligators, 14, 15
American alligator, 15
American white pelican, 15
American wood stork, 15
Anna's hummingbird, 15
Armadillos, 22
Attracting wild animals, 18–19

Barn owls, 20
Bats, 18, 21
Black bear, 14
Brown bat, 15
Bobcat, 15, 21
Bottle-nosed dolphin, 15

California gray whale, 20
California gull, 15
Canada geese, 9, 12–13
Carrier pigeons, 16
Cattle, 16
Cliff Swallows, 8–9
Clothes moth, 22
Cottontail, 15
Cougar, 10, 14
Coyotes, 10, 11, 19, 22

Deer, 22
Dogs, 6, 16, 17, 19
Domestic animals, 6
Donkeys, 16

Elephants, 17
Elk, 8

Falconers, 17

Gray fox, 15
Gray kangaroo, 15
Gray squirrel, 14, 18
Guide dogs, 17

Hanuman langur, 14, 17
Hawks, 10

Indian cobra, 15

Kangaroos, 10
Killer bees, 22

Mallard duck, 14
Manatees, 10
Mexican freetail bats, 21
Mice, 18
Migration, 8
Mission San Juan Capistrano, 8
Monarch butterflies, 9
Moose, 15
Mountain lion, 14

New South Wales koala, 14

Opposums, 11, 18, 19, 22
Owls, 18, 20

Partnerships
    between humans and animals, 16–17
Peregrine falcons, 6, 17
Pigeons, 6, 16
Polar bears, 9, 14–15
Puma, 14

Rabbits, 11, 18
Raccoons, 11, 18, 22
Rattlesnakes, 10
Red-tailed hawk, 14

Skunks, 11, 19, 22
Spiders, 18
Squirrels, 6, 14, 18
Striped skunk, 15
Swallows, 8-9

Turtles, 21

Wapiti, 8
Water buffalo, 14, 16
Western gray kangaroos, 10
Whales, 20
Wild animal
    definition of, 6
Wolves, 16
Wood storks, 21